somewhere only we know.

Ballads of unrequited love, loss and hope.

Abhyuday Kiran Hadal

Copyright © 2024 Abhyuday Kiran Hadal

Made with ♥ on the Notion Press Platform

www.notionpress.com

To Amma,

For always loving me beyond measure.

Contents

CONTENTS

Preface

Somewhere Only We Know is not just a title; it's a reflection of my personal journey through life and love's intricate paths. Written over the years as I have grown and navigated the world, these poems encapsulate moments of introspection, discovery, and the profound emotions that shape our lives.

While the heart of these poems draws from my personal experiences, their literary influences span a wide spectrum. Rooted in the timeless tradition of ballads yet embracing modern poetic forms, Somewhere Only We Know finds its voice through a blend of classic elegance and contemporary expression. Each verse is a tribute to the rich tapestry of poetic traditions that have shaped my journey as a writer.

This collection spans the emotional spectrum, delving into themes of love, loss, and hope. Each poem is a reflection of the myriad emotions that define our human experience—

capturing moments of tenderness, resilience, and introspection. Through these verses, I hope to offer readers a journey that resonates deeply with the universal themes that connect us all.

The writing process for this collection has been a journey in itself. Each poem within these pages has grown alongside me, evolving to reflect different phases of my life and emotions. What began as scattered verses gradually coalesced into a cohesive narrative, weaving together moments of personal growth and introspection. Somewhere Only We Know is more than a mere compilation; it is a testament to the cyclical nature of life and love, capturing the essence of my journey from inception to culmination.

As you journey through the pages of Somewhere Only, We Know, I invite you to find solace and strength in the poems within. Amidst the complexities of love and the ache of loss, these verses offer a reminder that there is always love and hope waiting on the other side.

May these poems resonate with your own experiences and inspire a sense of resilience and optimism, guiding you through the echoes of life's emotional landscapes.

Each poem in Somewhere Only We Know represents a phase of my journey thus far on this earth—moments cherished and challenges overcome. I hope that, like me, you will turn to these verses in moments of pain and sadness, finding solace in the memories of joy and the hope for the future they evoke. Through gratitude to God, these pages celebrate the grace that guides us through life's trials and illuminates our paths forward.

Thank you for embarking on this poetic journey with me.

Warm regards,

Abhyuday Kiran Hadal
12-07-2024

Spring Sun, Autumn Moon

O Autumn moon, you light up the dreary
rooms of my heart,

Your twinkling stars bless me with
companioned solitude and your cool gales
quench the eternal flame that burns me.

But the fulgent night fails to hide your silent
sorrow,

Autumn, I pity you

Have you ever loved?

You soothe the tears of many hurt lovers but
how have you the capacity to love?

Solitary in the dreadful tranquil night sky,

Is there a star you love?

Perhaps a wind you like?

Autumn, your sighs douse souls which are set aflame but I wonder if there is a hidden sadness within you.

Your radiant face enjoying the bliss of solitude like a lone teardrop in a vast emotionless face.

If no one, I have you and you have me, I promise I will come to you when I'm hurt but first promise to comfort me and offer respite.

After all the comfort and love offered by another sad lover is the best remedy.

So, let us rejoice in each other's company.

I love you for you understand me and pity you for you do not know love at all;

Abhyuday Kiran Hadal

So, I pray, answer me

Who is it that you love?

The translucent mists? Or the trees that yearn
for your gentle gaze?

I'm seething with anger don't you see? I do
not know, So, tell me, please tell me and if
you have no one take me, take me and love
me as you do to the nameless one.

I cannot confide in you, for I love you, but
the more I love the more it hurts, nevertheless
I finally understand.

I know who you pine for, someone you know
you will never see, whose beauty reaches you
only by the gossip of the stars.

I now truly understand why you heal others it
is because you know the unforgiving painful
sting of unrequited love.

To never be able to see the inscrutable beauty,
to never see the thing you have been
promised is indeed cruel.

But alas! You have me and I have you, so
forget the nameless one and choose me
instead,

Even if I'm merely a stand-in I wouldn't care,
let me experience your infinite love, give me a
chance to equal the nameless one and I
promise I shall deliver.

Sever your ties and take me,

Do not reject me and run.

But I know why you shall never accept me, it
is because,

Abhyuday Kiran Hadal

You love the Spring Sun.

Humanity's Last Ballad

Is there any beauty in human error?

Human mistakes are but malice guised with terror.

Sadness seeps and malice creeps.

But for love, humans will do anything and forget that divinity will reap.

Thousands of springs and winters too,

Humans are inept at forgetting lost love which is true.

Sand slips and the sun dips.

As sure as that, a human will surely trip.

Abhyuday Kiran Hadal

Rotting from the inside, does the true human malice reside.

It is a shame if anyone attends this world's masquerade without a mask and assumed beauty in their stride.

Understanding everything is lies; is truly a task.

Falsehood, pretence and betrayal mar the human soul.

And nature will definitely face the toll;

Of sin and sorrow and everything foul.

The tables turn and Gods pray for us all.

Morbid cold seizes humanity,

Shredding us of any last moments of serenity.

Biting cold and bone-chilling winds shall
ravage this world's tranquil bliss.

Where are the blooming roses now?

Buried within layers of doubt.

The clear springs have nothing but blood;

Rolling heads of innocents carried by the
flood.

The buildings sway with each passing day.

Birds don't sing, not anymore anyway.

Trees only sigh under the sun's burning glare.

Humanity cannot look up to God and stare.

Lost within the shrouds of time.

Deprived of anything positive and sublime.

Tossing and turning on the oceans of God.

Challenged by thunder, storms and clouds of sand.

Ripped from the inside from something remotely man.

Heavens can't save us now.

It can only be done by some 'thing' man.

Dandelions

With the reflection of the stormy skies in my eyes, you see beyond the frenzied grey obscurity and behold the dandelions that float carelessly in the sweet summer breeze of my heart.

The storm-brought winds fail to part the curtains of my heart, but your mere sight is enough to part my lips as well. What evil is in me to hate those who linger o'er you like flies to a fresh flesh wound, but I know of their intention to rot.

I have grown self-afflicting in the cold desolation of my lonely despair with not even pain nor anger as a company in my dreary solitude.

But I know you see the rainbow-winged butterfly that slumbers within me waiting to writhe into life and bring you healing. To gently caress your wound and bandage it with my name. And yet you prefer the flies for company.

I am encased in a cocoon of eternal winter bathing in my warm-bitter tears. The dandelions shed their seeds into the breeze of my heart waiting to reach you.

But beware the day I emerge as a radiant butterfly, floating gleefully in the sweet-summer breeze, drenched in nectar and bejewelled with pollen for only the heavens will know where you are then, within the grasp of death's still hands.

Staring at the sky with those lifeless eyes, yearning for the rain to clean you, for the butterflies to dance around you as they once did. But the grave choice you made has given you his gory end, rotting in a windless plain where the dandelion seeds cannot reach you, with only the flies as company.

Abhyuday Kiran Hadal

Feverish Fervour

What is this feverish fervour that I feel?

Which makes me so restless,

I feel the vehement flames deep inside my bones,

And yet I feel so cold,

The wisps of nostalgia whisper;

Reminding me of things I can never have,

The strings of fate entwine me in a single burning path,

Time fails to heal me, instead makes me hurt,

Deepening a hole as dark as the abyss and filling it with stones,

What is this feverish fervour that I feel?

It eludes me from sleep,

A pale flame grows inside, making me remember more and weep,

I yearn for the stroke that would free me from this dream,

That endlessly plays on,

I yearn for the voice as gentle as dew, telling me I'm loved;

What is this feverish fervour that I feel?

For a person long forgotten;

Whose voice fades by the caressing breeze,

Whose face is ephemeral,

Come heal me, come free me,

From this eternal nightmare,

I long for you, don't you see?

Come meet me even if it's in a dream.,

Happiness wanes just like the moon,

Reflecting on my woes, I beseech you to
please come soon,

Everything fails to console me,

Nothing feels special anymore,

The people who fawn over me, are nothing
but a bore;

You are the only one, who I've truly loved;

So come forth, show me your ardour,

And free me once more,

This is my prayer, a hymn for better days…

Abhyuday Kiran Hadal

Still

In the quiet mornings of February,

You descended upon me like a bouquet of
May flowers.

Your presence is spring itself.

When will you add me to your wreath?

Give me the ring.

How the rose got its thorns

The crimson blossom bit its tongue and fought back bitter tears,

Flustered at the sight of rainbow droplets that gently flowed off the red cheeks of a soul wounded with desire;

The soft sobs, choked gasps and sleepless nights of a bleeding lover suffocated the warm bud,

Its burning hue fading slowly with time,

For millennia the blossom bore infinitesimal proclamations of love but the loving flower confessed that

the anxiety, fear, nervousness and anticipation
were real,

The beautiful rose flourished to countless
blurred countenances to show affection but
not one asked the

flower if it could ever measure up to the love
it witnessed, no one asked if it could speak the
words the

lover wished to share,

Like a rag, it was passed from one hand to
another but the rose's pain grew deeper with
each new person that would hold onto the
flower brimming with expectations that the
flower knew it could not keep forever,

The meaning of love to the rose meant nothing;

For it knew it would only go from one hand to another but never to its own.

Nobody asked if the rose's heart lay elsewhere, it desperately cursed itself at the dawn of each new day,

Where a young lad would pluck it, rip it from its haven it called 'home'

And give it to his love,

Countless thorns grew where fruits should have been;

Eons of suffering and pain diminished its spirit and after enduring it all

Abhyuday Kiran Hadal

The rose finally lost its colour, a deep blue
seized its thorny existence,

The flower which once radiated warmth had
now gone cold;

And this is how the rose lost its colour and
got its thorns.

Mess

You float down the fleet of stairs, your feet almost untouching.

You wince at the moment your tender feet touch the hardwood floor,

Guided by nothing but habit, motivated by nothing but inexperience you amble through the darkness.

What you are looking for is anybody's guess, the rough silhouette that promises.

You sidle and swerve amongst the hoards of furniture, dodging each of them skilfully.

But alas, you smash your toe against the mahogany shelf, and everything goes to a blurring symphony.

You wake up wrapped in silk sheets, carried
by four shoulders. You cannot move and can
only observe what they do to you.

Time moves like jelly and your body moves
not. And all you can do is see, like a distant
echo amidst the treacherous fog at sea.

Cradled by silk that feels like craggy sharp
rocks. The sunny air feels so lost and cold.

Then they lay you to rest, the last teardrop
escaping your eye; A silent scream to bid
goodbye.

You see a light, a lighthouse perhaps?

But it feels warm, almost too warm to be true.
Then it burns your flesh right off your skin
and makes your pores bleed too, you can't feel
your legs anymore nor can you breathe.

Your screams are stifled and your mouth
sewed shut, at least your tears should offer
respite but your glands are sealed too.

The smell of all things foul floods your nasal
chambers. Burnt skin, hair and all things bare.

The light grows dimmingly bright and
suddenly there is nothing at all.

Only you and yourself, in the trance of a
never-ending fall.

Abhyuday Kiran Hadal

Stitched Heart

Touch my bruises, darling.

Do you feel my pain? Do you know why I'm crying? Because I don't.

It's not a cut but an affliction. That I have incurred in my cold desolation haunted by my visions of you.

I know your ghost, smiling through the smoke. Watching my wound grow deeper.

Do you miss the secret of us, hiding in the shadows, whispering promises and now how can you be so cold?

I gave you my all, I felt it. Now you treat me like I'm something expired and old.

Then let me expire, you are a false prophet who refuses to let me go in peace.

But you're the reason, who trespassed against me and committed treason.

You took me out piece by piece.

Now, pooled in red. I cry a river of blood. I want you dead and I want to be the flowers on your grave.

I love you and you made it hurt so bad. I lived the many lives that we could have, and now my only life lies shattered, a tombstone by your grave.

Save me, by a miracle. Stitch my heart. I'm begging you.

Abhyuday Kiran Hadal

Hues of Love

From the dusty windowsills and the old couple that sits in front of a deserted store,

Love flows like a gentle river through all of us, and we like stones are polished, shaped and glazed by the loving river.

Love is not a right and yet our bodies and minds crave it; muscles, tendons and bones aching to sleep beside the one we love.

Love has many faces, if love is one then forgiveness is the other. For truly can Love exist without compassion and forgiveness?

Poetry is Love in all its many forms, layered, and nuanced. From the day we are born, Love sleeps inside of us like a cocoon sheltered and untouched from worldly impurity waiting to burst forth like a butterfly.

This butterfly's flaps make the sound of poetry and its wings coloured in every shade of our soul.

Love is beautiful, golden threads that puppeteer us in unimaginable ways. All the love we throw out into the universe returns to us, often unexpectedly and mostly right on time.

But Love is sometimes suffocating, when the cloth called love is embroidered with the deep-blue infatuation and burning-red obsession, it is not a cloth anymore but a noose that tightens around the necks of those led to perdition.

True Love is like a bandage of flowers, sweet-smelling and healing. Its gentle warmth wrapping its arms around the loved. But Love is never enough, to change someone.

For the few lucky enough to drink from the golden fountain of Love, will tell you about the taste of Love. Its taste of all the beautiful things you can imagine, the taste of the moon, clear streams, mangoes, home and everything that offers respite to one's weary soul.

Home

Isn't it beautiful?

To experience it all

Within the nurturing confines of your walls,

From indignant protests and our first falls,

Now refusing into people who refuse to leave it all.

You have taught me all I know,

To see beauty in my sorrow, and joy in my woe.

And be prepared to face anything that comes tomorrow.

We have learnt to see in our fears a state of
grace,

And live our lives without counting the
number of days,

You have helped me find colour and sight as
we sail through this world of black and white.

You sacrificed your every need, to see me
succeed.

Isn't it beautiful?

That the simple joys we took for granted,

Are now the only things we realize we ever
wanted.

The time we spent running under the
scorching sun,

But who knew it would change our definition
of fun.

I will dearly miss these common memories we share,

I know you will too, because you care.

Isn't it beautiful?

How we taught each other, that if our skies were turning grey,

We need only paint it yellow and blue for another day.

We share a commonly special bond woven by threads of fate;

It is a bond strengthened by love and cannot be broken by something as weak as hate.

Our hearts bleed yellow and blue,

So, leaving you will take some time getting used to.

So finally, isn't it beautiful?

How three words can inspire and move you.

Abhyuday Kiran Hadal

Our hearts beat as one, ringing with "I love you"

Sciophyte

Under your shade, as cool as the shadow of an olive tree.

I can't leave but you want me to.

Don't push me, I beg.

The sun is burning me, I say. Don't push me off and you won't call it love.

I'll give anything to stop this feeling, I must stop the world.

I want to stay, till I'm dead and buried. Till my body buckles under the heat and I'm in the wooden casket that you carry.

My body is turning red with the fear of turning blue, without having you see how you look to me.

I can see the light, leaving my eyes.

And I try so hard to hold on and perhaps it
might not be so long before I'm gone.

But please, know that I can't love you any
more than I already do. I can't let you go, nor
can I suffer with this silent pain anymore.

Promise me when I rot, under your warm
shade. You'll finally know that I love you.

Forever and ever, you're always so far away.
But please let me stay.

Metamorphosis

What makes a city?

Is it iron that is the very foundation of the
heart?

Or the steely grit of humans who inhabit?

Fire tests gold and sufferings a woman.

What are the sounds you hear, you ask?

Should I say the joyful outburst of festivals?

The cacophony of construction?

Or the silent cries of a human wronged?

The sun sets low over the city, hiding behind
layers upon layers of dust.

There are no stars here except the bright ones
in the aspirations of the people.

No pure water except the ones shed in hiding.

What makes a city?

The infinite money that goes behind its
construction?

Or the manifestation of the dreams of
millions.

We go about our lives ignorantly,

Unbeknownst to us in silent corners of places
long forgotten, there lies a child covered in
dirt, and adorned with rags crying out to his
dead mother.

In hushed silences, women suffer at the hands
of men, and in clandestine corners, men are
told not to cry.

What makes a city?

The jubilant festivals?

The hawkers selling their vibrant sweets-
sticky and covered with flies.

Turmeric and vermillion heaped in piles in
unending rows along the bustling footpaths.

Loud music played by people knowing that in
some corner of their hearts hopefully these
loud sounds, if only momentarily will drown
the ceaseless cries of all those who suffer.

What are festivals, then?

Celebrations to hide our guilt?

To hide behind the safe corners of our four walls, refusing to think about those with no walls. Busying ourselves with tasks to no consequence just to forget that poverty has gripped half the city.

The neon lights that twinkle endlessly are but tears of God- for us, full of pity.

We will be rescued by someone who sees it all,

And has the courage to stand for those with no feet,

Speak for the voiceless,

And enlighten the blind,

In fact, this someone resides within all of us.

So, become the crutches of the oppressed,

Amplify the voices of those who silently suffer,

And become a beautiful butterfly, in shining armour.

Metamorphose.

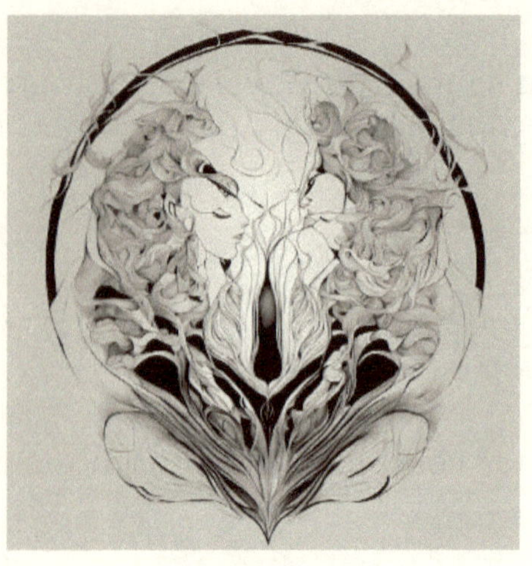

Abhyuday Kiran Hadal

Wishing Tree

When you smile at me, I blossom like the Gulmohar.

When you touch me, I shyly shed magnolia flowers.

When you look at me a certain way, I flush with lilac.

And when you wish upon me, I transform into a wishing tree

Mercy

You have two faces, vehement and foul. But also, pure and blissful like the mating call of a fowl.

Smiling and crying. On the border of madness. Confused whether to feel joy or sadness.

Yes or no? I wish you chose quickly. So, I can move on and thrust myself into the world for everyone to see.

A human without a mask at this parade of freaks. Waltzing through these crowds of ice.

One-half of my face chooses to play nice. The other just like you, wears a smug facade.

But inside it's writhing to leap onto trees like a
wood nymph- a dryad.

Your face lies incomplete, with flowers
growing out. Hyacinth, narcissus and all.

As life goes on, so must you for everyone
who wears two faces must finally fall.

True to no one but believes to be to
themselves. But the lies are two faces too,
they blur the distinction between false and
true.

Losing yourself within these shadows of
doubt, all that is left is all but nought.

Discover your face before the sands of time
run out, if you lose yourself, you'll struggle to
find out.

Falling for you

Standing at the cliff's edge and staring into the mirror-like waters that reflect my face, Is it the rain or my tears that ripple in that mirror?

Nosediving into the black waters that churn out frothy foam, and all I heard loudly above the crashing of waves was a simple song, a lullaby long forgotten perhaps.

I open my eyes to see dreary darkness all around me, the biting cold seizing my body.

But in the abyss below I saw a golden light calling out for me its burbling voice carried by the scarce bubbles that floated up weaving through shoals of brightly fluorescent fishes.

My body melted into the gentle darkness, sinking through like a hot knife to butter and yet above all that I heard a soft hum of a lullaby long forgotten.

The darkness embraced me and even though my closed eyes I could see as clear as day the warm light that radiated from the abyss, smile at me and reach out for me.

Is this love? Or a longing for something I have never had? Only below the earth's surface in solitude did I truly realize that it was light.

The very same light that could not break the impenetrable fortress I had resurrected around me before, now reached the recesses of my heart lighting it up and filling it with butterflies of warmth in the desolate darkness.

After the last bubbles of life left my lip and the last tear of resilience had slipped out of my eye merging into the dark waters, could I truly see the light when my eyes were closed forever.

Only in the most desolate darkness could light actually reach me and only when my eyes had closed forever could I truly see. The truth.

What matters in life is the symphony that weaves it together. The worst pieces weaved with the threads of hope, perseverance and love can make a beautiful dress.

This is the recipe for a beautiful life.

Escapism

Towards that blue sky, drenched in the sweat of God.

Pure and undefiled, like the cotton white west wind.

To a place where the wanderers belong. Where the colours are more colourful and the night sky even darker.

Let's go towards that blue sky, with a quiet tranquil bliss. Let us make sure we don't miss the cacophony of the city.

In each other's company, let us bloom unflinchingly and truly. Let us forget that thin metallic taste in our mouth that is so unruly.

With laughter and cheer. Let us run through the fields of sunflowers and marigolds. The flowers face not the sun but us for we shine brighter than it ever did. Each step into the ground making us sink further into our solitary bliss.

I promise that just as your river flows to the sea, my river shall flow to you and merge with you with my warm waters. Then I beg you to forget the sea, for we have an ocean of love for ourselves.

Let's walk on the wispy clouds, as soft as the promises we whisper to each other in the dead of night.

Let's fall from the clouds as they grow heavy with rain, just as our eyelids before we drift off into sweet slumber in our elegant embrace.

As we freefall, through the night sky. The breeze whipping against our faces and bodies seizing in the freezing cold. And yet it feels so warm.

Abhyuday Kiran Hadal

I want to melt in your arms alone, till the day that I die. And if I die, let me die first for I can't walk the path of night without you.

It feels so cold, I'm so lost without you. I reminisce about the forever that we had that was ephemeral.

Cushioned by the bare straws and cradled by the earth's arms. As we slept on the damp forest floor.

Beyond the world, beyond sadness. Eternal under the starry night sky. Each a diamond, a crystal tear escaping the eye of the moon.

We discover the universe is simply in each other's palm.

Fairy Tale

Once upon a time, my days would stand still as though waiting for your permission to begin unfolding.

And now, it is left in the quiet stillness of a ruin, unfrequented even by the indiscriminate rains.

Once upon a time, the smile lines and crow's feet creasing my face grew deeper with each passing moment beside you.

My face is bleary and streaked with coloured tears of red-hot anger and green jealousy.

When did we grow apart? Who was the cruel gardener who chose to rip us apart from each other and throw us into different fields?

My leaves now wilt in sadness, my fruits have gone dry. I have nothing to bear.

I see you dancing gleefully with the bees and butterflies. Golden, dusted with pollen and smelling sickeningly of nectar.

The water doesn't feel like it reaches me anymore. Why is the sun only shining on you? Do I deserve nothing?

Even the rains skip over me, and I'm shaded from the winds that you wave and float in with ease.

But in the dead of night, I smelled a fragrance. Sweet and silver almost dispelling the mist of night.

And then I looked at myself, adorned in stars, each a preciously crafted diamond delicately arranged on my body.

And that is when I understood, that the gardener of life was wise. He ripped me away from the parasite that superficially burned bright.

You were the red-rattle with no strength of your own, you made me, the Jasmine believe I was worth nothing without you.

But now I shine with a silver light, blinding everyone who shunned me. I burned for you, and you don't know my name.

To be close to you, I wanted to die. My foolish heart forgot to see the gardener protected me from harsh winds and shaded me from the burning sunlight. While you sucked the life out of another unsuspecting flower.

I'm worth everything, and I'll never forgive myself for believing what you sold me. But I'll try, for I love my scent.

Abhyuday Kiran Hadal

Wicked Game

I'll play by your rules one last time.

With rivers on fire, a strange world unfolds. I had never dreamed of the world you show me.

I don't want to fall in love with you.

With you, the forests rip apart in a psychedelic frenzy. You make me dream of you.

I don't want to fall in love with you.

Zipping through the night sky, silver we shine. Lost in the clouds.

I never thought I'd love somebody like you, and now I lost you.

I don't want to fall in love with you. Dream-catcher.

Blood

Nail me with a thousand needles,

Crucify me in your altar of love.

Drink my dripping blood, and rejoice in its
wine-like glory.

Smell the sweet scents that my body
permeates. Of pomegranate and primroses.

And then tell me, if that bitter aftertaste
remains after drinking from the fountain of
my crimson love.

In the mosaic of life, I am every one of the
missing pieces. I vow to fit perfectly in every
one of your blurred corners.

But don't shake me, don't treat me to your
silent treason. Because I'll give you a reason.

I am a storm with skin, there is such murder inside me. An all-consuming rage that will burn you to cinders.

And then I shall dance on the crisps of skin that you have left behind. I'll bathe in your dried tears and smear your ash on my body.

So, crucify me on the altar of your love. Before I rebel against you, my God.

But make sure to kiss me goodbye. Then I shall resurrect, red and pale.

Lily

Beside the bakery, smelling so sweet.

She lies silently there, mellow and bleak.

The dew condenses on her gentle lavender petals. And her smell becomes an earthy floral medley.

Crush her, and put her essence on me. Let me smell what it is to be free.

Not Mine

No matter what, are you not mine?

Don't leave, stay with me. Are you not mine?

With our fingers intertwined let us count the
stars that adorn the night sky. We'll teach love
the universal language that transcends identity.

In the evening sky, you reside. Haunting me
in my memories. Like an unfinished poem,
you linger on in my mind.

Aren't you mine? Why do you flow away like
the river that meets the sea? When the ocean
itself waits for you?

You need me, don't run away from me. You rescued me but I want to build a kingdom of fantasy ruled by our passions.

No matter what happens to me, you're mine.

Amma and I

My mother has golden-soled feet, engraved like the glimmering valleys of the Ganges, her skin is tinted yellow and her lotus eyes, are as playful as a deer in spring.

She strides amidst the plumes of dust buoyed by the rhythmic thumping feet of people vacillating from hawker to hawker. As I watched her barely lifting my nose from my book, My mother gave me an approving look.

She settles down, perching in an orderly line of women who have journeyed life midway. Their diaphanous saris were embroidered in gold-flecked grey. She joins them in crooning the same monotonous tune.

"Buy these bangles for your - Moon" tired uxorious newlyweds stop by, and say something about their wives catching them in a lie. They buy their gifts and leave- at least they tried.

But she sits there resolute, her sari covering her face, for who can withstand so much soot? She craves the few coins they throw at her, for who else would pay for my school year?

She's never held a pen in her life and yet she learned how to use a weighing balance with much strife. My Father only eats away at her finances and she is stuck in this never-ending dance, between selling and yelling and telling me that sugared flour in water is milk.

For now, coarse cotton saris should do, for how can she hope to have silk? Our leaders refuse to help her since that is what their mothers did and their grandmothers too. But she sleeps restlessly at night, with us, her malnourished kids in her bleary sight.
She makes a promise so loud yet so soft, whispering it to herself aloud. That she will make us touch the firmament's highest cloud.

Still, she asks herself, what about me? *"Am I not allowed?"* To dream about things so daring, yet the only thing she can do for now is scream.
For so long she has endured this sad fate, for me she has stayed strong and sacrificed everything without a debate. Rest, I tell her.

She closes her tired eyelids and drifts away into an unfamiliar world, she sits in the same lotus position on the cold, gravelly ground. The hawkers are nowhere to be seen, nor is there any sound.

She skims through the faces at the parade, and there she finds a little girl who looks like me, wan and wasted, exhausted by the vices' endless tirade but her sad eyes nestled in her sweet patient face, knocking at her heart's door.

All the subtleties like how the girl's *veil* covered any scintilla of skin from preying eyes, how the girl's bag was hung by the front to ward off unsolicited touches, gnawed at her heart with an unnamed longing.

"Is this worth going to school?" she asked, and the little girl in my likeness simply replied *"It's better than at home, used and thrown as my husband's tool"*

Healing Scars

River on fire, nobody could see me but you.
The haze of heat makes me desire a strange
world just for me and you.

The scars now feel like a distant dream, I
don't want to fall in love with the numb pain
and muffled screams.

Evil for someone to let me feel this way,
writhing and waiting. Like a wounded coiled
snake ready to strike, killing.

But when you talk to me, it feels like
lightning. Like a hidden rain from the blue sky
that hides in the cover of the rolling hills.

I'll burn down the sky for you, but I'll make
sure you burn too. Then let us dance this final

time, I warn you do not bet against me, not even a dime.

With you gone, I'll leave this identity and all these scars. I'll shed like a snake and emerge iridescent and new. And this time I'll hide and only give my heart to a select few.

In the pleasant summer heat, I'll come out to bask. To enjoy every moment that I live without you. With you gone, so is my mask.

Scars are faded now. Healing. But sometimes the pain returns at the dead of night and the urge to feel the numbness again. But I remember what a stupid reason, I won't commit this treason against myself.

I cry, not because it's not fair. But because for once I can cry without wanting to feel nothing. I feel the all the emotions now. Full and everything.

When I wake up without you beside me, the tears roll but so does a silent smile creep up from deep inside.

I only thank you, for giving me chance to stop this feeling. Now I only kneel before God and his justice.

Abhyuday Kiran Hadal

Endless July

Like the transient rains that come and go,

I pray that you don't go.

Stay with me forever, let us bloom together in
an Endless July.

Kisses

Faking a laugh, starburst to rainbows.

Let's dance on the horizons of memory and love.

I'm running away to somewhere romantic in the recesses of my mind. Join me, what do you say?

Fog and moisture on windows, scribbling hearts and initials. Flames and chance.

Prom and dance, is it always supposed to this slow? Can we not skip to the good part?

Taking our shoes off after a long day, when you get your arms around me it finally feels like home.

Wild and naive, I taste the anticipation and my gut churns. Faltering on fault-lines and expecting a tectonic shift.

The world comes to a halt, and the birds sing only for us. The trees sway in the breeze waiting for us. The stars stop and watch.

You know all the right buttons to push, you're falling through my fingers. You're all of my triggers.

But when our story ends, promise me we'll be happy, kisses.

Distance

A light year away, slow and unmoving I watch you.

Your laugh and movements.

But, I can finally turn away and be at peace.

Abhyuday Kiran Hadal

Close

Is it when I sit close to you?

Or when I laugh at all your jokes?

Does it make you happy? It's torture but it feels so good, it takes me all of my courage to talk to you.

I want to know what I look like to you, the only thing separating us is an ocean of pain.

My pulse races, will I get to talk to you today? Perhaps if I get lucky. But we're separated by a crowd of people each of them a wall made of gold.

I'll show you our future, give me your palm. September arrives soon.

I see better in the dark, so go ahead and turn off the lights. They didn't help anyways.

Horror movies and tea? I want to be alone but I can't bear to be, so will you keep me a lonely company.

You give my heart wings, promise me in the end everything will be worth it.

Abhyuday Kiran Hadal

Acknowledgements

Writing this book has been an extraordinary journey, and I am grateful to many people who have supported me along the way.

First and foremost, I would like to thank my family for their unwavering support and encouragement. My mother, Shilpa Kiran, and my father, Dr. Kiran, your love and belief in me have been my greatest source of strength. To my grandparents, Chandrasekhara and Jyothi, Kumar and Girija, your wisdom and guidance have always been a beacon of light in my life.

To my teachers, Deepa Sebastian, Odella John, Madhushree Baral, and Sheena Sam, thank you for always supporting my creative endeavours. Your encouragement and dedication have played a pivotal role in nurturing my passion for writing.

A heartfelt thank you to my friends and mentors, Gauri Nimbalkar, and friends

Tanushri, Sanath, and Aamina. Your companionship, understanding, and support have been invaluable throughout this journey. There are so many more friends who have been a part of this path, and I am deeply grateful to each one of you.

To every heart-break, pain and sorrow. For making me a stronger person.

Lastly, to the readers, thank you for opening these pages and embarking on this journey with me. Your engagement and reflection are what give these words life.

To Goddess Saraswati, Goddess of arts and poetry, thank you for guiding me and blessing me with the divine gift of creativity.

This book is dedicated to all those who strive for change, who believe in the power of words, and who find solace in poetry. Thank you for being part of this incredible journey

About the Author

Abhyuday Kiran Hadal is a 17-year-old author from Bangalore, India. Known for his profound literary talent, Abhyuday has been featured on UN Women YouTube and holds the distinction of being the youngest co-author published by Bloomsbury in the book "Unsung Valour: Forgotten Warriors of the Kurukshetra War." Currently in the 12th grade, Abhyuday has been writing since a very young age, showing a remarkable dedication to his craft.

He is deeply involved in youth empowerment and education, working with various NGOs and forums. Abhyuday also serves as the Co-Chair of Youth at the Arts and Culture Working Group. Despite his young age, this book marks his first significant publication, showcasing his journey as a writer.

Abhyuday's literary tastes are eclectic, spanning from Dostoevsky to Murakami, and from Sylvia Plath to Oscar Wilde. His love for reading is matched by his ambition to pursue a career in medicine and healthcare. To connect with Abhyuday, you can reach out to him on LinkedIn - <u>Abhyuday Kiran Hadal</u>.

somewhere only we know.